Collins English Library
Series editors: K R Cripwe

A library of graded readers for stud
native readers. The books are grad
idiom and sentence length are all c
in *A Teacher's Guide to Collins Engl
level. Level 1 has a basic vocabular
words, 3: 1000 words, 4: 1500 word
which are asterisked are accompani

Level One
- Inspector Holt and the Fur Van* *John Tully*
- Inspector Holt: Where is Bill Ojo? *John Tully*
- Crocodile! *K R Cripwell*
- Four Short Stories* *Margery Morris*
- Fast Money *K R Cripwell*
- It's a Trick! *Lewis Jones*
- The Story of Macbeth *from Shakespeare*
- Tin Lizzie* *Jane Homeshaw*
- Dead in the Morning* *Jane Homeshaw*
- Letters from the Dead* *Jane Homeshaw*
- Taxi! *Jane Homeshaw*
- The Pathfinders* *Jane Homeshaw*
- Inspector Holt: Cats in the Dark* *John Tully*
- Inspector Holt and the Chinese Necklace *John Tully*
- Journey to Universe City *Leslie Dunkling*
- Three Folk Tales* *Margaret Naudi*
- The Man with Three Fingers *John Tully*
- Fastline UK *Jane Homeshaw*
- The Grey Rider *Steve Rabley*
- Love Me Tomorrow *Jane Homeshaw*

Level Two
- The Magic Garden *K R Cripwell*
- Muhammed Ali: King of the Ring *John Tully*
- Inspector Holt Gets His Man* *John Tully*
- The Canterville Ghost* *Oscar Wilde*
- The Prince and the Poor Boy *Mark Twain*
- Inspector Holt: The Bridge* *John Tully*
- Oliver Twist *Charles Dickens*
- Two Roman Stories *from Shakespeare*
- The Titanic is Sinking* *K R Cripwell*
- The Wrestler *K R Cripwell*
- Madame Tussaud's* *Lewis Jones*
- Three Sherlock Holmes Adventures* *A Conan Doyle*
- The Story of Scotland Yard *Lewis Jones*
- The Charlie Chaplin Story* *Jane Homeshaw*
- Charles and Diana *Margery Morris*
- A King's Love Story *K R Cripwell*
- Dangerous Earth *Jane Homeshaw*
- Chariots of Fire* *W J Weatherby*
- Shark Attack *Jan Keane*
- The Complete Robot: Selected Stories *Isaac Asimov*
- Roadie *Chris Banks*
- The Mystery of Dr Fu Manchu *Sax Rohmer*

Level Three
- Climb a Lonely Hill *Lilith Norman*
- Custer's Gold *Kenneth Ulyatt*
- Gunshot Grand Prix *Douglas Rutherford*
- David Copperfield* *Charles Dickens*
- Born Free *Joy Adamson*

Five Ghost Stories* *Viola Huggins*
Three English Kings *from Shakespeare*
An American Tragedy *Theodore Dreiser*
Six American Stories* *N Wymer*
Emma and I *Sheila Hocken*
Little Women *Louisa M Alcott*
The Picture of Dorian Gray* *Oscar Wilde*
Maimunah *David Hill*
Marilyn Monroe *Peter Dainty*
Bruce Springsteen *Toni Murphy*
Is That It? *Bob Geldof*
Short Stories *Oscar Wilde*
A Room with a View *E M Forster*
The Importance of Being Ernest *Oscar Wilde*
The Lost World *Sir Arthur Conan Doyle*
Arab Folk Tales *Helen Thomson*
Computers: From Beads to Bytes *Peter Dewar*

Level Four
The White South *Hammond Innes*
A Christmas Carol *Charles Dickens*
King Solomon's Mines* *H Rider Haggard*
Jane Eyre *Charlotte Brontë*
Pride and Prejudice *Jane Austen*
Dr Jekyll and Mr Hyde* *R L Stevenson*
Huckleberry Finn *Mark Twain*
Landslide *Desmond Bagley*
Nothing is the Number When You Die *Joan Fleming*
The African Child *Camara Laye*
The Lovely Lady and other Stories *D H Lawrence*
Airport International *Brian Moynahan*
The Secret Sharer and other Sea Stories *Joseph Conrad*
Death in Vienna? *K E Rowlands*
Hostage Tower* *Alistair MacLean*
The Potter's Wheel *Chukwuemeka Ike*
Tina Turner *Stephen Rabley*
Campbell's Kingdom *Hammond Innes*

Level Five
The Guns of Navarone *Alistair MacLean*
Geordie *David Walker*
Wuthering Heights *Emily Brontë*
Where Eagles Dare *Alistair MacLean*
Wreck of the Mary Deare *Hammond Innes*
I Know My Love *Catherine Gaskin*
Among the Elephants *Iain and Oria Douglas-Hamilton*
The Mayor of Casterbridge *Thomas Hardy*
Sense and Sensibility *Jane Austen*
The Eagle has Landed *Jack Higgins*
Middlemarch *George Eliot*
Victory *Joseph Conrad*
Experiences of Terror* *Roland John*
Japan: Islands in the Mist *Peter Milward*

Level Six
Doctor Zhivago *Boris Pasternak*
The Glory Boys *Gerald Seymour*
In the Shadow of Man *Jane Goodall*
Harry's Game *Gerald Seymour*
House of a Thousand Lanterns *Victoria Holt*
Hard Times *Charles Dickens*
Sons and Lovers *D H Lawrence*
The Dark Frontier *Eric Ambler*
Vanity Fair *William Thackeray*
Inspector Ghote Breaks an Egg *H R F Keating*

Collins English Library Level 2

THE MAGIC GARDEN

K R Cripwell

COLLINS
E·L·T

© K R Cripwell 1977

Published in Great Britain by
William Collins Sons and Co Ltd
Glasgow G4 0NB

Printed by Martin's of Berwick

All rights reserved. No part of this
book may be reproduced, stored in a
retrieval system, or transmitted in
any form or by any means, electronic,
mechanical, photocopying, recording or
otherwise, without the prior permission
of the Publisher.

First published in Collins English Library, 1977
Reprinted: 1983, 1984, 1985, 1987 (twice),
1989 (twice), 1990

ISBN 0 00 370081 X

Illustrations by Mike Cole

Contents

Akantown	7
God's Money	9
The Pumpkin	15
The Cold Eyes of Mr Ngwenya	19
The Bride Price	25
The Back-of-the-Moon Bar	31
The Game of Cards	34
A Happy End	41
Some Questions	46

Akantown was not a beautiful place.

Akantown

Akantown was not a happy place. Most of the people were very poor. They worked in the big town twenty kilometres away. Every day early in the morning they went by bus and train. At the end of the day they came back to their homes in Akantown. On Fridays they took their money home with them.

Akantown was not a beautiful place. Its people did not have good houses. Only a few houses were stone houses. Most people made their houses out of old boxes and paper. There was no water in the houses. The women carried water to their houses on their heads. In the houses people had only two or three chairs and a table. They cooked out of doors because there were many fires inside the wood and paper houses. Life was hard in Akantown.

But on Fridays people were happy. There was music and the people sang and danced and drank in Akantown.

Kumalo ran towards the church.

God's Money

Kumalo was one of the poorest people in Akantown. He had no work in the big town and no money. He sat in the sun all day with his brown hat over his eyes. He thought about food and drink and a beautiful house. He thought of many other things. But without money he could have nothing.

"I must get some money," he thought. "Without money for food and drink I'll die. I must find some money. Yesterday I found an orange but one orange is not enough. I must have money for a lot of oranges. I must buy a lot of food and drink or I'll soon die."

But Akantown is a very poor place. People with money hide it carefully.

"I'll ask God for help. I must go to the church. God must help me now."

Kumalo ran towards the church. It was on a small hill. There were no houses near it. A road full of small stones went up to the door.

Kumalo took the money from the bag.

Now Kumalo walked slowly. He could hear the people in the church. They were singing together. It was Sunday.

He opened one of the big doors a little. He looked inside and saw Father Gashle.

"You must not steal," Father Gashle said. "God says this. You must never take other people's things. That is wrong. They do not belong to you. That is the word of God."

Kumalo sat down at the back of the church.

"Now let us sing," said Father Gashle. The people began to sing. Father Gashle gave a bag to a man at the front. The man took some money from his pocket and put it in the bag. The money was for the church. The man then gave the bag to a woman next to him. She put some money in the bag also. Then the bag came to Kumalo. He held the bag in his right hand and opened it slowly. He saw the money. There was a lot. He touched the money with his finger.

"God has answered me. He has given me all this money. I will never go without food and drink again."

The people came to the end of the song. They sang, "Aaaaa . . . men."

Kumalo took the money from the bag and put it in his pocket. He put the bag behind some books. Without a sound he opened and closed the church door. He began to walk slowly down the road from the church. Just then he heard

Father Gashle inside the church.

"Stop thief! Stop thief!" shouted Father Gashle. Then the people began to shout, "Stop thief! Stop thief!"

Kumalo looked back. The two big doors opened with a loud noise. Father Gashle came first. He was very angry. Behind him came the people and they were very angry. They shouted, "Stop thief! Stop thief!"

Kumalo began to run. Kumalo was strong and he could run very fast. The people from the church were old and tired. They could not run very fast. Father Gashle was very fat. But he ran faster than the others. All the time he shouted, "Stop thief! Stop thief!"

Kumalo ran in and out of the houses. But the people from the church and Father Gashle did not stop. Other people heard the story of the thief in the church. They also began to run after poor Kumalo. Kumalo now began to run slowly. He was tired.

"What can I do?" he thought. "I must put the money in a safe place now. Then I'll come back and get it tomorrow. I must not lose God's money." Just then he saw a vegetable garden behind a small house. In the garden grew a very big pumpkin. He had very little time. He made a hole in the ground under the pumpkin and put the money in the hole. Then he put the pumpkin over the hole. "Stay there,"

In the garden grew a very big pumpkin.

he said. "I'll come back for you tomorrow."

The people soon found Kumalo. Two big men held Kumalo. Father Gashle looked in all Kumalo's pockets. There was nothing. They couldn't find the bag with the money on him.

"Where have you put it?" asked Father Gashle. "You are wrong," said Kumalo. "I never took a thing. It must be another person."

Father Gashle and the people were not very happy. Father Gashle said, "We must let you go now. But we are all going to keep our eyes on you. We don't want a thief in Akantown." Slowly the people went back to their houses.

Kumalo sat down under a tree. "I am going to keep my eyes on that pumpkin," he said very quietly.

The Pumpkin

Mrs Olusanya had four children — Abraham, Mary, Ruth and Naomi. Mr Olusanya was dead. They were very poor. Mrs Olusanya worked in the big town. She cleaned the houses of rich people there. She brought some money home every Friday. But there was never enough money for food. Now it was only Sunday and already there was no money. She and her children looked at the empty table.

"What am I going to do?" she thought.

Then she remembered the pumpkin in the garden. "Abraham, go and cut the pumpkin in the garden. It is very big. We can eat some of it today. We'll have a little of it every day. We'll have enough food for a week."

Abraham took a knife from the kitchen. He went into the garden. He turned the pumpkin over and began to cut. Then he saw the hole and the money.

"Mother! Mother!" he shouted.

Mrs Olusanya and the three girls ran out into the garden. Abraham held the money in his hands. "I found it under the pumpkin," he said. He gave the money to his mother. There was a lot of money—fifty dollars!. The girls began to sing and shout, "It's a magic garden. It's a magic garden!"

"Let us give thanks to God," said Mrs Olusanya. For a short time the girls were quiet. Then they began to shout again. "It's a magic garden. It's a magic garden."

From under the tree Kumalo kept his eyes on the money.

Mrs Olusanya said, "There's enough money here for food. We won't be hungry for a long time. Now I must go to the shop. Come children." She held the money in her hand. "We're going to buy enough food for all of us."

The family walked down the road to the shop. Mrs Olusanya did not go to the shop very often. She never had enough money. But today was different. She had a lot of money. She called out to her friends, "I'm going to the shop. We're not going to eat only pumpkin this week. I'm going to buy lots of things at the shop."

"Where did you get the money?" her friends asked.

"In the magic garden," the children shouted. "Under the pumpkin. Abraham found it."

"God gave it to us," said Mrs Olusanya.

Abraham held the money in his hands.

"He gave us a magic garden."

In a few minutes all the people in Akantown were in their gardens. They all wanted a magic garden too. Children dug, old people dug, mothers, fathers dug. The dogs dug too. But they did not find another magic garden.

The Cold Eyes of Mr. Ngwenya

But Kumalo saw all. He kept his eyes on the money in Mrs Olusanya's hands.

Mrs Olusanya went to the shop. It was Mr Ngwenya's shop. He was not a very kind man. His shop was the only one in Akantown. So the things in his shop were often very expensive. It was Sunday but the shop was open.

"Good morning, Mrs Olusanya, what can I do for you?" asked Mr Ngwenya. His face was happy but his eyes were cold.

"I want a lot of things, Mr Ngwenya. I want. . ."

"How are you going to pay?" he asked.

Mrs Olusanya showed him the money in her hand. "Is this enough?" she asked.

Mr Ngwenya opened his eyes wide. Fifty dollars is a lot of money and he wanted it all. With all that money Mrs Olusanya could go to the big town. She could buy everything there because the shops there were cheap.

"She must spend all the money in my shop," he thought.

"That's a lot of money, Mrs Olusanya. You can't spend it all at once. Give it to me. I'll keep it for you. That will be easier for you. All the best people in Akantown do this. Now what do you want?"

Mrs Olusanya stood for a moment. She thought, "Mr Ngwenya is a kind man. He'll keep my money because I can't hide it in my house. Every Saturday I can come to the shop and buy my food without money."

She said, "Thank you, Mr Ngwenya. I'll give you the money. Here it is."

Then Mr Ngwenya gave Mrs Olusanya a letter. It said: Mrs Olusanya gave me fifty dollars today. She bought food for ten dollars. I must give her forty dollars next Saturday. At the end of the letter was Mr Ngwenya's name and the date.

Mrs Olusanya bought her food. At the door of the shop she saw Kumalo. "Haven't I seen him before?" she thought. But she could not remember.

As the family walked home the girls sang softly, "It's a magic garden. It's a magic garden."

In the shop Mr Ngwenya was happy. He took the money in his hands. He looked around the shop. The young man was no longer at the door. Mr Ngwenya always hid his money carefully.

Mr Ngwenya always hid his money carefully.

There was a hole in the floor under a heavy box. He moved the box and put the money in the hole. Then he heard a noise. "Who's there?" he called out.

There was no answer. He called again. But again there was no answer. He took a heavy piece of wood and went to the door of the shop. There was nothing there. "It must be a thief at the back of the shop," he thought.

He ran through the shop into the back room. He looked carefully but there was nothing. He came back to the shop. Then he remembered the money in the hole. He looked down but the money was no longer there. He ran out of the shop and shouted again and again, "Thief! Thief!"

Then he saw Kumalo. He remembered the young man at the door. He must be the thief.

Kumalo was the thief.

"Stop thief!" shouted Mr Ngwenya. "There he is. Stop him and I will give you twenty dollars! Stop thief!"

Twenty dollars is a lot of money in Akantown. Soon many people were in the streets running after Kumalo again. "There he goes," they shouted.

What could Kumalo do now?

Then he saw a bicycle beside a wall. So he jumped on it and rode away.

But many other people had bicycles too. Kumalo rode in and out of the houses. But he could not get away. "I must hide the money again," he thought. "But I can't stop. Where can I put it this time?"

James sang. It was a very sad song.

The Bride Price

James Nkulumo and Jenny Hove were under a big, old tree in her uncle's garden. Two birds sang in the tree. They were in love. James and Jenny were also in love.

James sang. It was a very sad song. He wanted to marry Jenny. But Jenny's uncle wanted a hundred dollars for a bride price. Jenny's mother and father were dead. Jenny's uncle was her mother's brother. She had no other family.

"Young men must always pay money for a good wife," said Jenny's uncle. "They must save money for a bride price. So you must give a hundred dollars to me. Without this money you cannot marry Jenny. Jenny is a beautiful girl. So her bride price is a high one."

But James did not have a hundred dollars for Jenny's uncle. He had fifty-four dollars but that was not enough. So the two young people were sad. And the song was a sad one too.

He threw it high into the big old tree.

Just then Kumalo rode by on his bicycle. The people on bicycles were very near now. Kumalo looked behind him. He could not see them but he could hear them. Their shouts were very angry. He took the money out of his pocket. He threw it high into the big, old tree.

James began his song again. The paper money began to fall around the two lovers. One dollar note fell on Jenny's hand. She closed her fingers on it and began to play with it. She touched James on the arm.

Suddenly James stopped his sad song. "What have you got in your hand, Jenny?" he asked.

"Only a leaf from the tree," she said. Then she looked at the leaf in her fingers. It was not a leaf; it was a one dollar note. There were lots of other dollar notes on the ground around them. And many more were still in the tree. James climbed into the tree and Jenny looked in the grass. Soon they had a lot of money in their hands.

"How much have we got?" James asked.
"Fifty dollars," answered Jenny.

"Fifty and fifty-four makes a hundred and four dollars. We have enough for your bride price! Now we can marry. Let's find your uncle."

"Oh happy day," sang Jenny.

"Oh magic garden," sang James.

Together, hand in hand, they ran from the garden into the house. "Where is your uncle,

Jenny?" James asked. "Uncle is at the Back-of-the-Moon Bar," she answered.

But what has happened to Kumalo?

Not far from the big, old tree the people on bicycles stopped Kumalo. They took him to Mr Ngwenya because they wanted the twenty dollars for Kumalo.

"That's him. That's the thief. He stole a lot of money from my shop."

"But I never stole any money," said Kumalo. "Look in my pockets. You'll find nothing. Mr Ngwenya is a bad man. You all know that. He steals a little from all the poor people in Akantown. I'm a good man. I don't steal. Ask Father Gashle. He'll tell you. Fifty dollars is a lot of money. Perhaps Mr Ngwenya has stolen it from some poor person."

The people did not like Mr Ngwenya. Perhaps Kumalo was right and Mr Ngwenya was the thief. Soon Kumalo was free again.

Kumalo walked slowly back to the big tree. On the way he met James and Jenny. They shouted to him, "We can marry at last. We have enough money for the bride price." They showed Kumalo and their other friends the money.

"Where did it come from?" their friends asked.

"Out of the big tree," said James.

"Out of the big tree in our magic garden," said Jenny.

Soon all their friends were in the garden under the big tree. But there was no money there. Only the two love birds at the top of the tree. They ran to their gardens and looked in all the trees. But they did not find another magic garden.

She was old, but she was still beautiful.

The Back-of-the-Moon Bar

The two lovers ran on to the Back-of-the-Moon Bar. Behind them came Kumalo. He kept his eyes on the money in James' hand. It was a lot of money. Now there were a hundred and four dollars. He could buy a lot with all that money.

The Back-of-the-Moon Bar was the biggest building in Akantown. Inside there were a lot of tables and chairs and it was very dark. It was Sunday. But there were many people in the bar. At one table there were four men. They had cards in their hands. There were bottles on the table. Three or four men sat at each of the other tables. Some men drank quietly. Others shouted for food and drink. Pretty girls brought drinks to the tables. There was a lot of noise in the bar. You could hear the music all over Akantown.

At the back of the room stood Miriam. She was old, but she was still beautiful. She had a red mouth and black hair. Her dress was long and black. You could see her long legs through her dress. She had a happy smile but her eyes were cold and hard. The Back-of-the-Moon Bar belonged to Miriam.

The two young lovers ran into the bar. They looked for Jenny's uncle among the men. But the room was very dark. Then Jenny saw her uncle. He was alone at a table.

"Uncle! Uncle!" Jenny called out. "We have the money for the bride price. Can I marry James now?"

The noise in the bar stopped at once. Everybody knew the story of the bride price.

Jenny's uncle stood up. James came up to him. His face was so happy. "Here is the bride price, uncle." He put a hundred dollars in the uncle's hands. James kept four dollars in his pocket. He was going to give these to Father Gashle. They were going to get married in Father Gashle's church.

"Father Gashle is going to marry us today," Jenny said.

"Where did you get all this money?" asked Jenny's uncle.

"Out of the big old tree," said Jenny.

"God sent it to us," said James.

"God gave us a magic garden," said Jenny.

All the people began to talk at once.

Jenny's uncle looked at the money in his hand. He looked into the eyes of the two young people. "You have paid the bride price," he said. "Now go. Find Father Gashle. He can marry you today."

All the people in the bar shouted and banged the tables. There was a lot of noise. Some of the girls began to cry. Not one of them had enough money for a bride price. "We'll never get married in Father Gashle's church," they thought.

"Thank you, uncle," said Jenny, "Come, James. Let's find Father Gashle. He will marry us at four o'clock this afternoon. All of you must come."

The Back-of-the-Moon Bar was a happy place that day.

Miriam called the bar girls. "Give a bottle to every person in the bar. Take no money. It is free. I am giving this because of this happy day."

Again the men shouted and banged on the tables. They drank fast and ran out of the bar. Soon the bar was empty. Each wanted a magic garden for himself. But not one of them found a magic garden that day.

The Game of Cards

Only Miriam and Jenny's uncle were in the bar now. Miriam had her eyes on the money in the old man's hands. She did not see Kumalo in the dark. Kumalo also had his eyes on the money.

"Uncle, this is a happy day for you," said Miriam. "Jenny is going to marry today. James is a good man. They will be happy together. You will see. I know."

Miriam came up to the old man. She put her hand on his arm. "Have another drink," she said. "It is now three o'clock. Stay here with me. Then we can go together to the church."

Jenny's uncle was an old man. He had no wife or children. Only his sister's child, Jenny. And now she was going from him. She was going to live with James. The old man was very sad. He began to cry.

"Be happy," said Miriam. "It is always like this. Children grow. Then they fall in love and marry. They are like the birds in the trees. They soon fly away."

The old man took a drink from the bottle. Her kind words made him a bit happier. He did not see the hard face of Miriam. And he did not see Kumalo in the dark.

"Let's play a game of cards," said Miriam. "It will soon be four o'clock."

Jenny's uncle liked cards. He played every day in the Back-of-the-Moon Bar. He played for money. But he often lost and Miriam knew this.

"Yes, why not? Sixty minutes will go quickly. Then we can go together to the church."

Miriam brought the cards to the table. "Shall we play for money?" she asked.

"Yes, why not?" answered Jenny's uncle.

They began to play. The old man won a lot of Miriam's money in the beginning. He was very happy.

But then slowly he began to lose. Miriam's cards were always better than his. She always had the high cards in her hand. She began to win all the old man's money. He could not understand it.

But Kumalo understood. He could see Miriam. She had a lot of cards in her bag. They were all high cards. The old man looked at his cards all the time. Then Miriam put the high cards in her hand and the low ones in her bag.

Kumalo kept his eyes on her hands. She was a thief. "She has stolen the bride price from the

35

Miriam put the high cards in her hand and the low ones in her bag.

old man," he thought. "I must stop her now."

It was the last game. The old man had no money in front of him. "I have lost it all," he thought. "What am I going to do now?"

Miriam put the last few dollars in her bag. Her face was hard. She said, "It's four o'clock. Are you going to the church? I'm not. I'm too tired."

Kumalo stood up quietly. They did not see him. He grabbed Miriam's bag.

"Stop thief!" shouted Miriam.

"Stop thief!" shouted Jenny's uncle.

They ran out of the bar. "There he is. Stop thief," they shouted.

Kumalo held the bag in his hand. He ran and ran. But he was tired. He ran up the hill towards the church.

Mrs Olusanya heard the noise. She saw Kumalo. She remembered his face. He was the young man at Mr Ngwenya's shop. Then she saw Miriam. Miriam shouted, "Have you seen a young man with a brown hat? He has stolen my money."

Mrs Olusanya said, "Yes, He's gone that way. I'll help you. Come, children."

Mrs Olusanya, Abraham, Mary, Ruth, Naomi and Miriam ran after Kumalo. After them came Jenny's uncle.

All the people in their gardens saw Kumalo. They saw Miriam and Mrs Olusanya's family. They began to run after Kumalo. They shouted,

"Stop thief! Stop thief!"

Miriam saw Mr Ngwenya outside his shop. They were old friends. She told him the story. He remembered Kumalo. He grabbed a big piece of wood. He too ran after Kumalo.

Kumalo was very tired now. He could see the church at the top of the hill. He could hear the noise behind him.

Now the men from the Back-of-the-Moon Bar were behind him. They had stones in their hands. They shouted at Kumalo, "Stop thief! Stop thief!"

The girls from the bar were also there. They shouted at Kumalo.

Then the people on bicycles heard the story. They also began to ride after poor Kumalo.

The people from the church heard the story of Kumalo. "Yes, he's the thief. He stole the money from the church this morning," they shouted. Then they too ran after Kumalo.

Kumalo could see the doors of the church. His feet were on the stones of the road now. Kumalo put his hand on the church door. He looked behind at all the people. He looked at Miriam's bag.

What was he going to do?

He looked behind at all the people.

Kumalo opened the door of the church.

A Happy End

Kumalo opened the door of the church. At the other end he saw Father Gashle. In front of him were Jenny and James.

"Father Gashle. Help me. I stole the money this morning. Here it is. Please take it back," Kumalo ran to Father Gashle. He put the bag in his hands.

Just then all the people arrived at the church door.

Miriam shouted, "There he is. That's the thief. That's my bag. He stole my money."

Two big men held Kumalo by the arms.

"Is this true, my son?" asked Father Gashle.

"Yes," answered Kumalo. "I stole her bag. But she stole the bride price from Jenny's uncle. I saw her. Look in her bag. You'll see."

Father Gashle opened the bag. Inside was a lot of money. Then he found the low cards. Kumalo told the story of the card game.

"You are a bad woman. Why did you steal

from an old man? You are the thief, not Kumalo." Father Gashle took the money out of the bag. "How much was the bride price?" he asked.

"A hundred dollars," answered James.

"Where is Jenny's uncle?" asked Father Gashle.

"Here I am," said the old man.

"Here is the bride price — a hundred dollars."

The old man took the money. He looked at it in his hand. Then he looked at Jenny and James. He was very happy. Father Gashle gave Miriam her bag and money.

Just then Mr Ngwenya shouted, "Kumalo stole from me. He stole fifty dollars. He's a thief."

Father Gashle looked at Mr Ngwenya.

"When did he steal this money?"

"This morning."

"Where from?"

"My shop."

"But where in your shop?"

Mr Ngwenya did not answer. He did not want to tell all the people of Akantown about the hole under the box.

The people began to talk. They did not like Mr Ngwenya. He took all their money. The things in his shop were too expensive. He was a thief.

"Did you see Kumalo in your shop?" asked Father Gashle.

"No, but he was at the door."

"But he didn't come inside," said Mrs Olusanya.

"Ah!" said the people.

Mr Ngwenya said nothing.

"But now," said Father Gashle to Kumalo, "where is the church's money?"

Kumalo looked down at his empty hands. Where was he going to find fifty dollars?

"Take this," said Jenny's uncle. "How much do you want? I don't need all this money."

"Of course not, uncle," said Jenny. "You're going to live with James and me."

Jenny's uncle held out the money to Kumalo. "You're a kind and good man. You have a good heart."

Kumalo took the money. He gave fifty dollars to Father Gashle. He gave fifty dollars back to Jenny's uncle. Jenny's uncle turned to James and Jenny. "Take this," he said. "You'll need it."

Father Gashle looked at the fifty dollars in his hand. The church needed this money. He put his hand on Kumalo's arm. "Thank you my son. You heard the voice of God. Never be a thief. Now I am going to marry James and Jenny."

All the people of Akantown were happy now.

Miriam looked at Mr Ngwenya. Their eyes were cold and their faces hard.

And Kumalo? He found a good home with Mrs Olusanya. After all, two magic gardens in Akantown is enough.

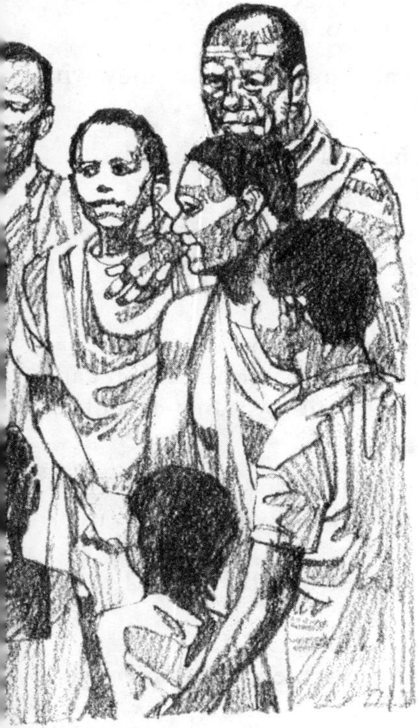

Find some words

We've hidden some words for you. Would you like to find them? Have a look at this sentence:

This book is called "The Magic DANGER".

The last word in the book's name is really *garden* — but we've changed the places of the letters. Here's another one:

In church, Kumalo touched the money with his FRINGE.

This time we've changed the places of the letters in the word *finger*.

Now perhaps you'd like to try some yourself. There are 19 of them. Find the right word every time.

At the end, write down the *first letter* of every answer. You'll have 19 letters. You can read them — they tell you the name of a place. What is it?

1. Many people went to town by INTAR.
2. The women of Akantown carried water on their SHADE.
3. People went to the big town LAYER every day.
4. Kumalo jumped on a CECIBLY.
5. The people in church ended their song with "NAME".
6. People with money hide it LACELYFUR.
7. The big town was a number of

46

MILKOTREES away. *kilometers*

8. LYON a few houses were stone ones. *Only*
9. There were many FRIES in the wood and paper houses. *fires*
10. Kumalo WERTH the money in a tree. *threw*
11. Most people made USHOES out of boxes and paper. *houses*
12. Mr Ngwenya sold EVENSIXEP things. *expensive*
13. Mrs Olusanya's girls thought their garden was CAMIG. *magic*
14. Kumalo: "Yesterday I found a GOANER, but one is not enough."
15. Mrs Olusanya said Kumalo stayed DETIOUS the shop.
16. The people ran after Kumalo with a lot of SIONE.
17. Jenny's RIBED price was a high one. *Bride*
18. When Kumalo took the money, Father Gashle was GRAYN. *angry*
19. Mrs Olusanya suddenly BREEMMERED the pumpkin in the garden. *remembered*